SPOT THE DIFFERENCES

BY
STEVEN ROSEN

■ SCHOLASTIC

ISBN-13: 978-0-545-08213-6
ISBN-10: 0-545-08213-7

10 9 8 7 6 5 4 3 2 1   08 09 10 11 12

A Quirk Packaging Book
Interior design by Nancy Leonard and Steven Rosen
Cover design by Becky Terhune
Photo editing and retouching by Steven Rosen

Printed in the U.S.A.   40
First printing, July 2008

You can Spot tHe DiffErencEs!

Welcome to the fun of spot-the-differences picture puzzles! In this book, you'll find twenty-four different puzzles to solve. There are four chapters—one for each season of the year. Each puzzle shows you two pictures that appear to be exactly the same—but if you look closely, you'll start to see some differences between the two. Check out that striped hat: are the colors the same in both pictures? Look at the clock on the wall: what time is it in each picture?

At the top of each puzzle page, you'll find the number of differences to look for and a difficulty rating. Answers are shown on pages 45 through 48—no peeking!

SNOWFALL

Bundle up to find these changes.

1
2
3
4
5

A   B   C   D   E

Answers on page 45

DOWNHILL

Don't fall down on this one.

☞ **8 changes**

👁 **CHALLENGING**

👁

6 WINTER

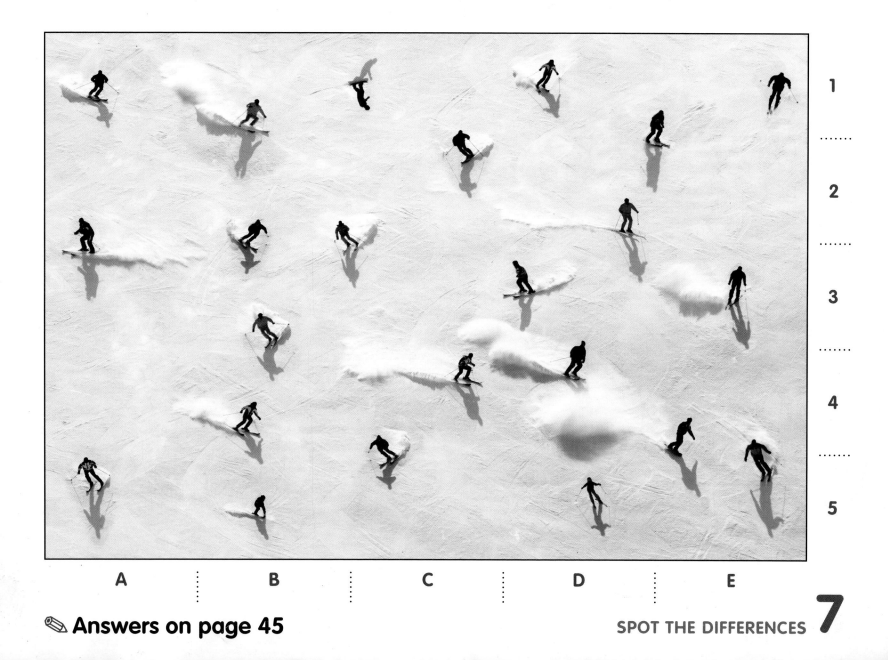

1

2

3

4

5

A   B   C   D   E

✎ **Answers on page 45**

SPOT THE DIFFERENCES **7**

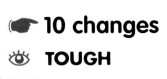
CHINESE NEW YEAR

Don't let these dragons drag you down.

1

2

3

4

5

A   B   C   D   E

✎ **Answers on page 45**

SPOT THE DIFFERENCES **9**

TAKE A BITE

A crunchy cookie puzzle for you.

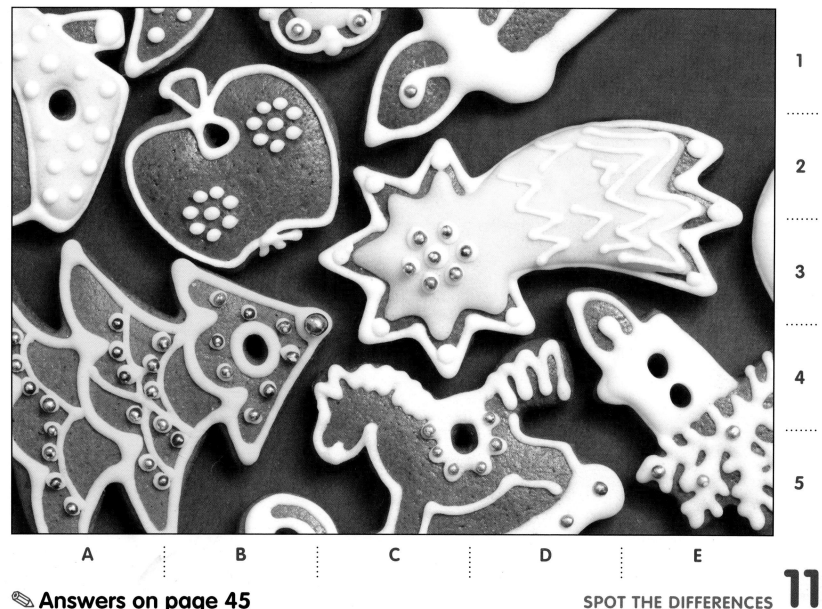

1

2

3

4

5

A   B   C   D   E

✎ **Answers on page 45**

Can you unwrap the differences?

1

2

3

4

5

A   B   C   D   E

Answers on page 45

SPOT THE DIFFERENCES **13**

HOLIDAY FUN

Crack this nut!

1
2
3
4
5

A   B   C   D   E

14 WINTER

✎ **Answers on page 45**

5 changes

EASY

How many changes are floating around?

1
2
3
4
5

A   B   C   D   E

✏ Answers on page 46

GIDDYUP

Go around to see what's changed.

6 changes 👉

EASY 👁

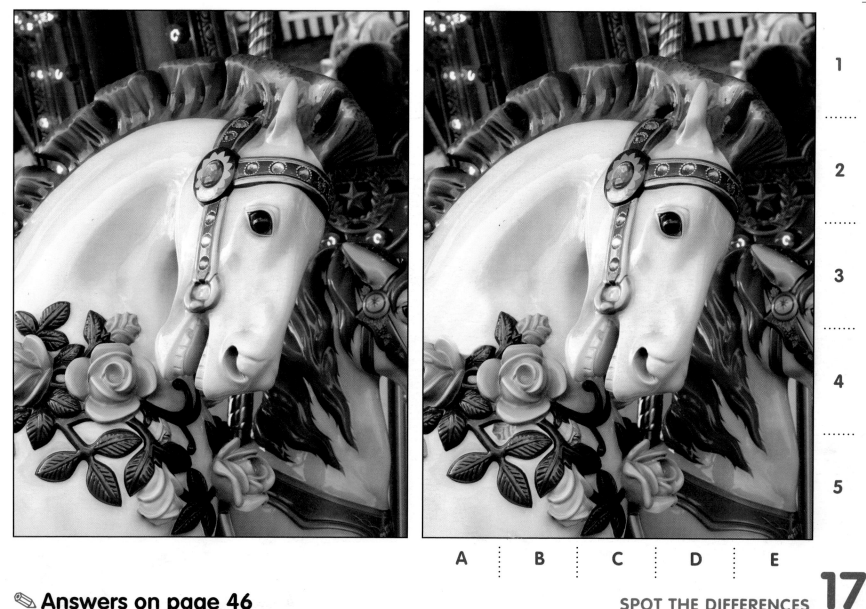

1

2

3

4

5

A B C D E

✎ Answers on page 46

SPOT THE DIFFERENCES 17

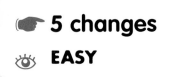
BLOOMSDAY

How's your flower power?

1

2

3

4

5

A B C D E

✐ **Answers on page 46**

SPOT THE DIFFERENCES **19**

👉 10 changes

👁 TOUGH

👁

👁

BUTTERFLIES FLUTTER BY
Find the differences before they fly away.

1

2

3

4

5

A   B   C   D   E

✎ Answers on page 46

SPOT THE DIFFERENCES **21**

☞ 7 changes

👁 CHALLENGING

👁

EGGS-TRA FUN
Scramble to solve this one.

1

2

3

4

5

A   B   C   D   E

✎ **Answers on page 46**

SPOT THE DIFFERENCES **23**

CLIMB HIGH
Grab hold of these changes.

☞ 8 changes

👁 CHALLENGING

👁

1

2

3

4

5

A   B   C   D   E

✎ **Answers on page 46**

HAVE A BALL

Let this one bounce around your brain.

1
2
3
4
5

A   B   C   D   E

✎ Answers on page 47

PALACE IN THE SAND

Can you build it?

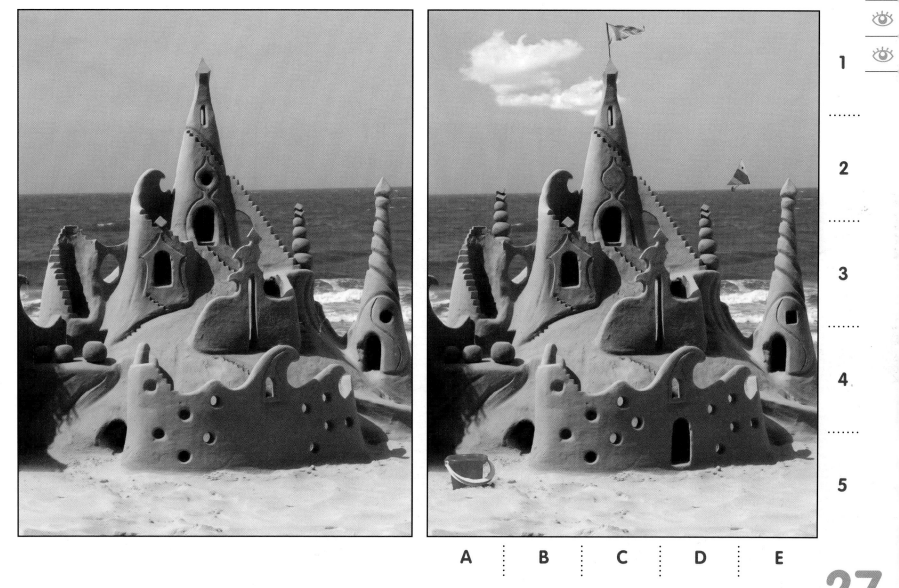

A   B   C   D   E

Answers on page 47

SPOT THE DIFFERENCES **27**

BOUNCE ALONG
Hop to it and solve this one.

1

2

3

4

5

A   B   C   D   E

✎ **Answers on page 47**

SPOT THE DIFFERENCES **29**

MAKE A SPLASH
Race to find the answers.

1

2

3

4

5

A   B   C   D   E

✎ Answers on page 47

SPOT THE DIFFERENCES **31**

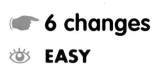
POOL PARTY

Dive on in.

1
....
2
....
3
....
4
....
5

A   B   C   D   E

✎ **Answers on page 47**

PLAYROOM

Make a game of spotting these differences.

1

2

3

4

5

A   B   C   D   E

SPOT THE DIFFERENCES **33**

TRICK OR TREAT

Don't let this one scare you.

9 changes

TOUGH

1

2

3

4

5

A   B   C   D   E

Answers on page 48

SPOT THE DIFFERENCES **35**

PUMPKIN HEADS

Fall into this puzzle.

1

2

3

4

5

A B C D E

✎ Answers on page 48

SPOT THE DIFFERENCES **37**

SCHOOL SUPPLIES
Can you supply the answers?

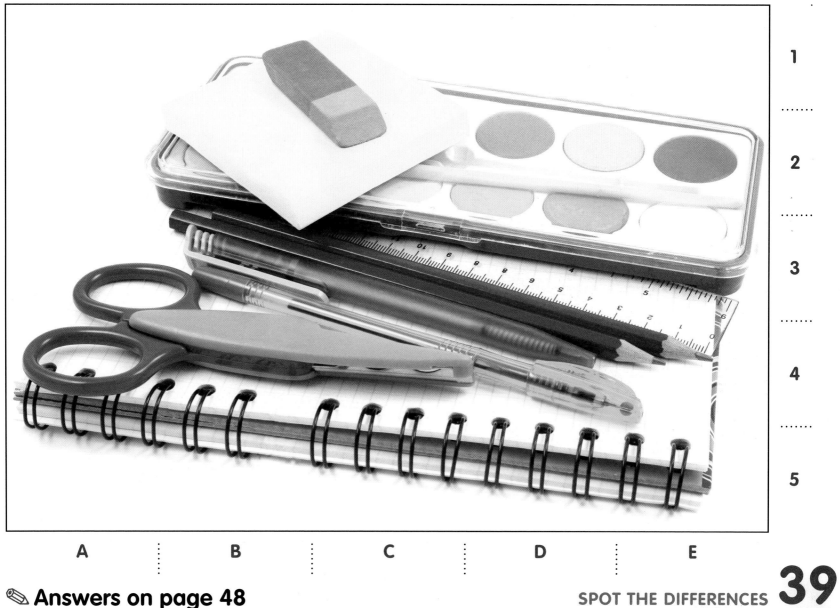

1

2

3

4

5

A   B   C   D   E

✎ **Answers on page 48**

SPOT THE DIFFERENCES **39**

AUTUMN LEAVES
Don't leave till you find the changes.

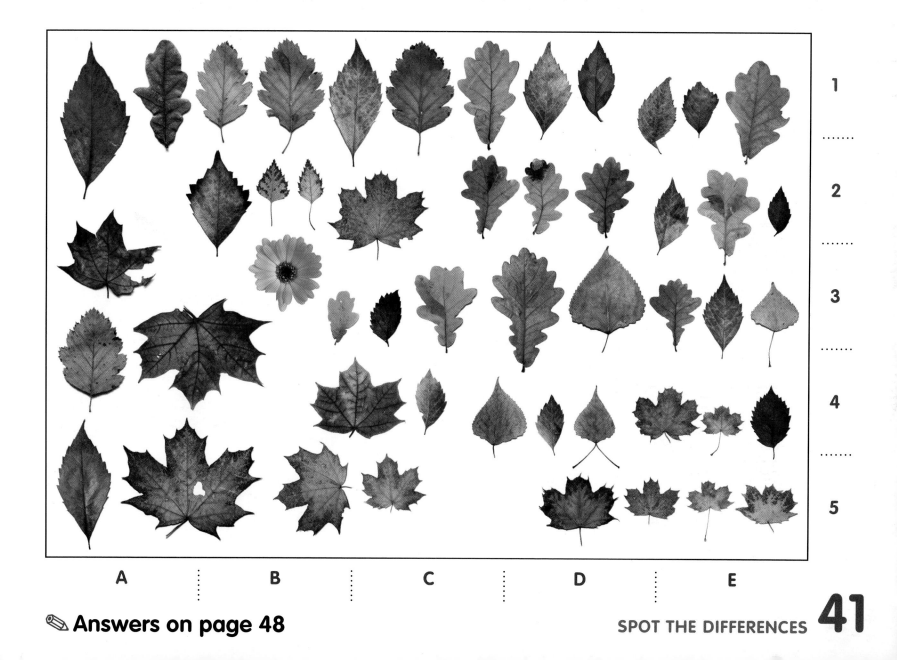

1

2

3

4

5

A   B   C   D   E

BACK TO SCHOOL

Don't read too much into this one.

1
2
3
4
5

A   B   C   D   E

✐ Answers on page 48

HARVESTTIME

Let this one grow on you.

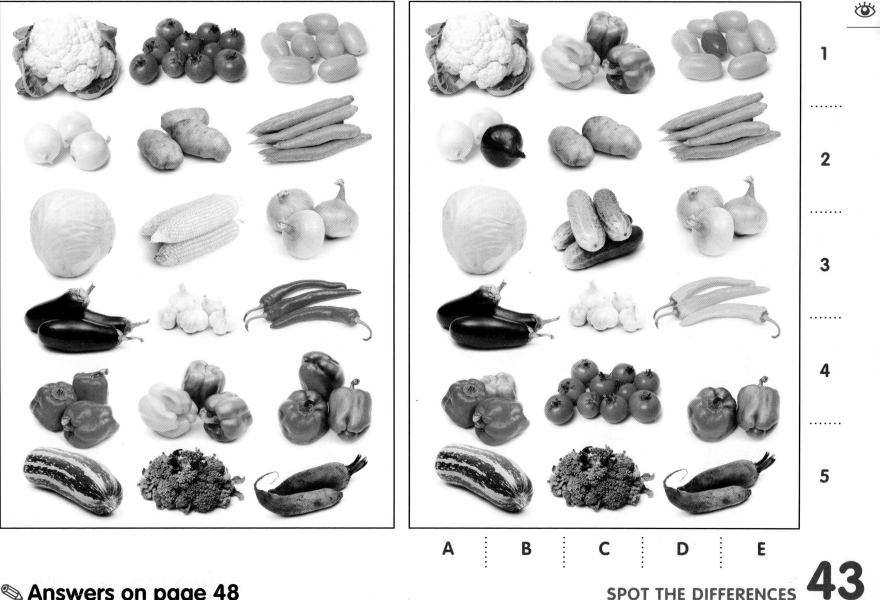

1
2
3
4
5

A   B   C   D   E

✎ Answers on page 48

SPOT THE DIFFERENCES **43**

ANSWERS

44

Winter

Page 5: Snowfall
A1: Yellow cord missing. C4: Two boards on toboggan joined into one. A3: Pom-pom missing. B3: Green stripe added to hat. D2: Ponytail missing. D3–D4: Orange stripe missing from right-hand glove.

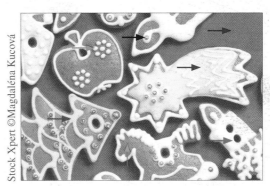

Stock Xpert ©Magdaléna Kucová

Page 10–11: Take a Bite
C1: Silver ball added to tip of candle. E1: Cookie missing. B1–B2: Extra dot design on apple. D2: Hole missing in tail of shooting star. A4–B4: Frosting now pink. C4: Horse's eye missing. E4: Extra hole in candlestick.

Page 6–7: Downhill
B1–C1: Skier upside down. D2: Snow spray missing. E1: Shadow missing. B2: Skier added. D2: Orange coat now blue. A2–A3: Skier going in opposite direction. E3: Snow spray missing. A4: Skier missing.

istockphoto ©Kristian Sekulic

Page 12–13: Gift Giving
D1: Star missing from hat. B2: Stars on hat now green. B3: Red ribbon now yellow. D3: Blue ribbon missing. B4: Blue ribbon now on other side of package. D4: Bracelet missing. D5: Shirt now purple.

Page 8–9: Chinese New Year
B1: Feather on top of dragon now yellow. C1, E1: Dragon's eyes now red. D1, E1: Black-and-white pom-poms now red and black. A2, C2: Dragon's eyes now green. B2: Third pom-pom added to nose. B2: Pink stripe missing from nose. D2: Nose now green. D4: Tooth missing. D4: Tongue now blue. D5–E5: Strings under chin missing.

Lucky Oliver ©Alysta Company

Page 14: Holiday Fun
C1: Feather on hat now green. D1: Ornament now silver. A2: Gold ornament missing. B3: Shoulders now blue. C4: Extra X in square on coat. B4–B5: Two buttons now on belt. C4: Button on coat missing. A4–B4: Stripe on sleeve now red. C4: Design on belt buckle missing.

SPRING

istockphoto ©Steve Krull

Page 16: Up, Up, and Away
A1: Hill missing. B1: Dots removed from yellow balloon. C1: Balloon added. B3: Pink marks in center of blue balloon missing. C5: Boat on bottom missing.

istockphoto ©Dave Logan

Page 17: Giddyup
C1: Light missing. C2: Pattern around stone now blue. B2: Blue stone now yellow. A3: Three leaves missing. B2–B5: Yellow rose added. D5–E5: Pink detail now blue.

istockphoto ©Beata Becla

Page 18–19: Bloomsday
B3: White flower now yellow. C5: Blue and white pot now pink and white. D3: Center of flower now yellow. D4: Leaf added to pot. A1: Petal removed from flower.

istockphoto ©Bershadskyy Yurig

Page 20–21: Butterflies Flutter By
B1: Blue and black butterfly missing. Yellow butterfly now blue. A2: Black turquoise butterfly replaces orange butt C2: Spots added to big white butterfly. D2–E2: Butterfly body now yellow. C Caterpillar added. D3–D4: Orange butt replaces black and turquoise butterfly. Half of butterfly missing. C5: White d added to bottom of blue and black butte D4–E4: Antennae missing.

istockphoto ©Slawomir Jastrzebski

Page 22–23: Eggs-tra Fun
A4: Green stripe missing. B4: Green dots now red. B4–C4: Ribbon missing. C4–D4: White egg now yellow. D4: Baby chick in egg. E4: Egg upside down. E5: Stick missing.

Lucky Oliver ©Ivonne Wierink

Page 24: Climb High
A1: Black stone added to wall. C1: Knot moved up on rope. C1: Orange circle missing. A2: Red circle now square. C2: Hood now yellow. B4: Designs on sneaker missing. D4: Yellow stone missing. E5: Orange circle now green.

Summer

Page 26: Have a Ball

A1: Red ball now blue. B1: Center of star now green. E1–E2: Red and black triangles now alternating. B2: Red star on top of ball. C3: Green triangles now pink. C4: Ball turned upside down. E4: Green circle added to top of ball. A5: Black outlines filled in. D5: Stars removed from red ball.

Page 27: Palace in the Sand

B1: Cloud added. C1: Flag added. D2: Sailboat added. A2–B2: Turret added. C2: Round window missing. E3: Round window now square. C4: Round window added. D5: Door added. A5: Pail added.

Page 28–29: Bounce Along

A1–B1: House now pink. B2–C2: Extra pane added to window. B3: Door now blue. C1: Plane added. A4–B4: Dandelions added. D3–E3: Stripe added to shirt. D4–E4: Circle added to ball. E1–E2: Telephone pole missing.

Lucky Oliver ©Gert Vreg

Page 30–31: Make a Splash

D1: Number 8 now 9. B2: Number 6 missing. D2: Strap missing on red bathing cap. E2: Yellow bathing cap now blue. E2: Red lane divider in back missing. E5: Yellow rubber ducky added.

istockphoto ©Marzanna Syncerz

Page 32: Pool Party

E1: Plane added. C2: Palm tree missing. D2: Beach ball upside down. A4–B4: Boy's bathing suit now orange. C5: Pail now purple. E5: Hole in girl's bathing suit missing.

istockphoto ©Galina Barskaya

Page 33: Playroom

C1: Clock now at 6:00. D1: Yellow ray missing. E1: Skylight missing. A2: Portrait of baby now faces in opposite direction. B1–B2: Number nine on clock now a three. E3: Cover of dog book now blue. C4: Center drawer pull added. E4: Drawer pull on top drawer missing.

AUTUMN

istockphoto ©Jani Bryson

Page 35: Trick or Treat
A2: Tiara missing. C1: Pom-pom added.
D2: Nose now blue. A3–B3: Belt missing.
B3–C3: Collar of shirt now green.
A4–B4: Eyes on jack-o-lantern solid
black. D4: Face missing on jack-o-lantern.
E3–E4: Tail missing. B5–C5: Flowers on
shoes now yellow.

istockphoto ©Jim Jurica

Page 36–37: Pumpkin Heads
D1: Third flower added to hat.
D2: Eyes now green. D2–D3:
Nose smaller. B3: Flower on
hat missing. D3: Tooth added in
mouth. B4–C4: Eyebrows
missing. D4: Turtleneck now
blue. A5: Extra button added.

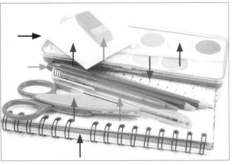

istockphoto ©Monika Adamczyk

Page 38–39: School Supplies
A2: Handle on paint box missing.
B2: Sharpener missing.
C2: White stripe on eraser missing.
D2–E2: Green paint now yellow.
D3: Number 7 on ruler now 8.
B3–C3–D4–E4: Red pencil now
blue. B4: Yellow dot on scissors
missing. B5: Spiral missing from
edge of notebook.

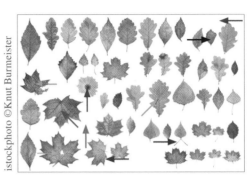

istockphoto ©Knut Burmeister

Page 40–41: Autumn Leaves
D1–E1: Red leaf now green.
E1: Horizontal leaf missing.
A3: Hole in leaf missing. B3: Flo
replaces leaf. A3–B3: Leaf upsid
down. D3: Yellow leaf now red.
B4: Small yellow leaf missing.
D4: Extra stem added. B5: Hole
added to leaf. B5: Leaf turned
on its side.

Lucky Oliver ©Thomas Perkins

Page 42: Back to School
B1: Orange replaces apple. B2: Green book
edge now red. D3: Little girl's bracelet
missing. D3: Book in girl's hand now green.
D3–E3: Backpack now green. D5: Flower on
shoe missing.

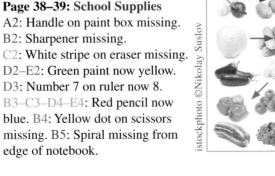

istockphoto ©Nikolay Suslov

Page 43: Harvesttime
C1: Peppers replace tomatoes. D1: One
yellow tomato now red. B2: One white onion
now purple. C2: One potato missing.
C3: Cucumbers replace corn. D3–D4: Red
peppers now yellow. B4: Green pepper
replaces red pepper. C4: Tomatoes replace
peppers. E4: Pepper missing.